Remarks On Existentialism: The Will to Conform

Jack R Ernest

Copyright

First Printing: January 2023

ISBN: 978-1-4478-6181-2

Foreword

I consider these notes an extension to my initial notes (Remarks On Existentialism: Boredom, Anxiety and Freedom.) I would strongly recommend that the reader reads "Boredom, Anxiety and Freedom" first before they attempt to read this set of notes. I felt compelled to write a literary sequel (if you can call it that) because I felt I had not fully analysed the philosophy in Boredom, Anxiety and Freedom. I see these notes as an addition to Boredom, Anxiety and Freedom and as such they are not an actual structured book. It stands to reason that if in the future I conceive of a new angle or philosophy with regards my existential theory I will write a third selection of notes on the subject.

With this set of notes, I discuss in more detail labels and interpretation along with finding one's existential freedom. I also refer to education and love, two elements which I regret I did not discuss in my previous notes. This is the third edition of these notes.

I also wish to apologize in earlier editions for singling out the female gender for criticism with regards love. What I was really attempting to assert was that stigma plays a huge role in why we wish to be in a relationship. It may have appeared that I was being sexist, when truly I was attempting to point out from a sociological perspective how the threat of being labelled negatively impacts both the male and female with regards to choosing to be in a relationship

Introduction

Where there is pattern in life there exists method behind that
pattern. There cannot exist nearly eight billion people on this
planet who all behave in identical ways without some
psychological force at work. In my opinion what sculpts
society to behave as it does is The Will to Conform. This is
the combination of evolution, education, the herd and the urge
to avoid boredom that inflicts conformity on the human being.
In every country and in every culture, you can observe
similarity. One focal point of this similarity is education.
Children around the world are systematically and collectively
educated so that they will mature into citizens that behave a
certain way and require certain things. Are people moral
because they are inherently moral or are they moral because
they are programmed to be moral? In my opinion it is the
latter. Through education and through the power of the herd
that can observe us, the individual wilts to the power of
conformity. In doing so they accept the life of careers and
relationships. What man truly fears in life is not violence but a
soiled reputation. In particular he ventures into the real world
to be labelled positively by the herd, which in turn makes him
feel good. He ties his self-esteem to being endorsed by
society. This is the psychological bind that shadows every
man and woman of this planet. There are problems however
with this system. One such problem is that man stakes his
happiness on relationships and careers. He attests that he
cannot be accomplished in his existence until he is married
and working in a suitable job. Thus, he never truly becomes

happy. He doesn't because he either fails to meet the stipulations of conformity or he does meet them but must maintain them in order to continue to be happy.

Now I recognise that this is just my opinion and that the reader may differ, but if man really wishes to be happy, he would be advised to live in solitude. If one can make themselves happy in the loneliness as opposed to being dependent on another person, they will discover a happiness that cannot be taken from them. In my humble opinion the despair we call being alone can actually ignite one's soul. If one can free themselves of addiction in life and become one with the universe, they will find in themselves a happiness that is stubborn and lifelong. One must transform their addiction to gratification into an attitude of gratitude. Make being alive the greatest quality of your life. I try with these notes and previous notes to convey to the reader just how people are manipulated to conform, and I offer a means to escape this implicit conformity.

The Will to Conform

Evolution   Education

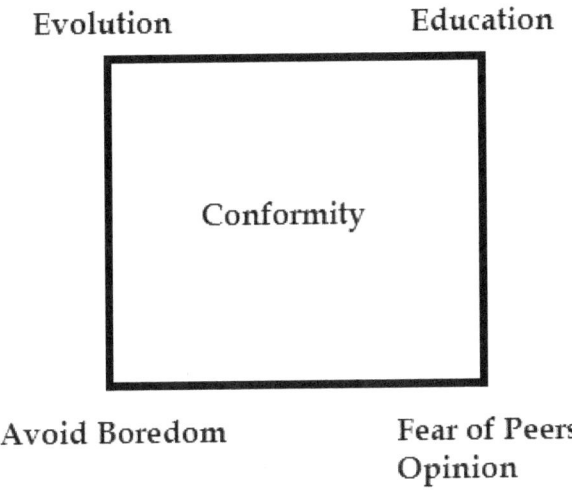

Conformity

Avoid Boredom   Fear of Peers
                             Opinion

1.0 The Will to Conform is the unconscious encumbrance that an individual is put under to conform. It is the invisible force that chisels man into who he becomes.

1.1 We have an idealistic dream of how our lives should be. We dream of relationships and careers. We think that if we have both, we should become happy. This is the power of conformity.

1.1.1 Furthermore, people who do meet the constraints of conformity are sometimes left disappointed and unhappy and they cannot understand why. The reason is that one cannot obtain happiness in life consciously.

1.1.2 For example one cannot say they will be happy for the next two hours. They will not be happy. What they can only do is immerse themselves in life and hope they become happy. Similarly, one cannot attest that marriage or a career will make them happy. All they can do is become married or work in a job and anticipate that happiness will be provided, but it is not certain.

1.1.3 This is the disease of conformity. We automatically think that it should make us happy. We assume that marriage and a stellar career will make us happy. It is however by no means certified.

1.2 Life causes so much distress and yet instead of retreating from it, we absorb ourselves in it, harnessing further distress. We are told this is how we should live but this model of living creates friction in our psyche. People through education have been bred to live only one way and know of no other means to live. The Will to Conform is strong in people and seldom does an individual violate it.

1.3 The Bind of Conformity: Through education and evolution we are automated to want precise things from life. But in gaining them we put ourselves in a bind. Education endeavours to make us chase friendships, relationships and work. Evolution implores us to hunt procreation. In achieving these things and in order to maintain them, we must conform. This creates anxiety. In order to work we must accept the stress that comes with it. In order to yield from friendships, we must take on the burdens that accompany it.

1.4 We conform unconsciously and that is why we are frantic to marry. Furthermore, we grow up under coercion from parents and friends and they incite us to marry, so as to follow in their footsteps.

1.4.1 A problem arises because one is in a bind. The Will to Conform battles on one side and the want to do as one wishes battles on the other side.

1.4.2 Furthermore people instinctively wager their happiness on conformity (marriage and work). They fully expect that adherence to those principles will generate happiness. This is wrong. Conformity may make one happy, but it may not.

1.5 People also fail to grasp that to deal with another person always carries the threat of uncertainty. People are by default unpredictable. They have their own opinions and interpretations. Thus, a healthy relationship will always involve chance as to whether it succeeds or not.

1.6 Both men and women's lives centre around relationships and marriage. From adolescence they have determined their life.

1.7 We are so caught up in relationships and careers that the horrors of this world go unnoticed.

1.8 We conform because we are programmed to find the result of conforming enjoyable. This stems from indoctrination of childhood. When young we were put in a room with our peers and we learned that them being impressed with us made us in turn feel good. We carry this mentality into adulthood. A computer has a system by which it operates. So too does civilization and it is called conformity. This is the cult that is exercised by the majority.

1.9 The herd mentality is so strong. The Will to Conform is borne out of fear.

1.10 All people are is breeding machines for economies.

1.11 We are all the same. We all have the same worries, the same anxieties, the same aspirations and the same dreams. This planet is home to probably the most intelligent species in the universe and yet we all behave identically. Men and women want a relationship and want a career. But the power of the herd is so strong. Ultimately, we are afraid of the very people we love.

1.12 We become so fearful of societies opinion. This stems from indoctrination through education. We become dependent on others for sociological exoneration, but we also fear losing their respect.

1.13 The modern-day man and woman are under severe hardship to be the modern-day man and woman. They do not realize that ideas are being planted in their minds on how they should behave and what they should want. They do not see the invisible wave of confinement that the herd puts them under to be retrospective men and women.

1.14 There are homeless men who are more enthusiastic of their existence than many men and women.

1.15 People are being manipulated to an extent. Every day they are told how to conduct themselves. What to choose and what not to choose. The rebel or the criminal who defies the herd is labelled accordingly.

1.16 We are radicalized on conformity. Just as a religious extremist is persuaded to murder innocent people in the name of his god, the law-abiding citizen is conditioned to conform.

1.17 The failure to conform is the fulcrum of many a woe. It is a mistake to do so, but so many measure their self-worth in conforming and when they fail, so too does their mental health.

1.17.1 We get told how to live and when we fail to meet the standard, we become agitated. We elope into others but often this escape causes stress. We are told that we must be around others in order to be content but being around them causes anguish.

1.18 This is the madness. This is the insanity. But because the majority fosters and encourages it, we become so seduced by it. People are so inured on the system, so brainwashed that they cannot see that they are part of a system.

1.19 Education has us dazed on people. We cannot live without them and we cannot live with them. Furthermore, we stigmatize the solitary individual and in doing so we set fire to any freedom we may ever have. You can be happy alone. You can find your inner peace in the solitude. But you must be prepared to deride your family and friends.

1.20 The cult of conformity is awesome. We are brainwashed not to question the system. If you look at planets or galaxies you see pattern. If you look at nearly eight billion people on this planet you see pattern. What socio-economic forces are at play?

1.20.1 Furthermore the individual recoils in horror at the thought of the purposeless of the world. They cannot fathom a duty-less existence. So where do they draw their duty from? They find it through religions, through love, through friendships, through sports franchises etc. They find their duty through conforming.

1.21 The laws are fabricated to incentivise conformity. People are incentivised to get married and to work. It is an ideology that society has accepted, and it is one that society is forced to accept. Capitalism like communism enforces a methodology of living on people. But why does capitalism succeed while communism fails? One reason is that people are overtly told how to live under communism whilst they are covertly instructed how to live under capitalism.

1.22 Anything that deviates from conformity is immediately considered cancerous. A person who fails to meet the stipulations of The Will to Conform is taken by anxiety. People are brainwashed into determining what is right and what is wrong. A progressive society allows people to make choice. It enables them to repel The Will to Conform.

1.22.1 The herd mentality provokes fear in the mind of the individual. That he works or has friends motivates him to conform. The more one associates themselves with the herd, the more they unconsciously are stressed into adopting the herd's ideology.

1.22.2 The herd is not necessarily a group of people. It can also be one person like a partner or friend and when we gain approval from them, we feel good.

1.23 The man or woman with a struggling marriage is in a bind. They both have become so disciplined on relationships that the option of going alone is not viable. Thus, they try their luck at another relationship hoping to be positively gratified.

1.24 We are caught in the jaws of the herd. When they ratify us, we feel good; but when they dismiss us, we feel bad. Thus, men try to be successful and women try to be attractive purely to earn the endearing eye of the herd. Ones liberty thus is invoked through fleeing the herd.

1.25 People are brainwashed into behaving a certain way. They ascertain that the meaning of life is to fall in love and build careers. The result of this adherence is a thriving economy. They are consumed by The Will to Conform. They have been indoctrinated from youth. How you perceive life is determined by the penitentiary you grow up in.

1.25.1 If a member of society looked at a religious fanatic, they would ascertain that he has been brainwashed. Now apply that to most of society. Through education they have been radicalized to behave a certain way. They believe in love and believe in working for an economy. They engross themselves in starting families and maintaining friendships. They have been brainwashed themselves.

1.26 Reality is the illusion, it is the hallucination. What if I told you society as we understand it is the delusion? What if working and relationships are the madness? That this world as we know it is the insanity that we have come to accept as normality. The real world is the universe. Relationships and careers is an illusion. It is the hallucination.

1.27 An example of the power of conformity is this: Take a stroll through a busy city street and you will see pattern. You will see that most women have long hair in comparison to their male counterparts. Now try to comprehend what pressures are at work that stimulate most women to have long hair? The answer is the combination of the herd, her family, her friends and the desire to be attractive etc. Now apply that to everyday life. And the dynamism is unconscious. The female never says I am going to have long hair to abide by the herd or to placate her friends and family. She simply has long hair because the decision is unconscious in its fabrication.

1.27.1 Another example is when we drive a car. We do not consciously attest that we will keep within the rules of the road when driving. No one says to themselves prior to driving: "I will try and drive safely." They simply drive safely unconsciously. They drive safely because they are programmed instinctively to do so. They stop at traffic lights, keep to the correct side of the road and put on their indicator at junctions because they have been trained to do so. Now apply that mentality to relationships, friendships and careers. We chase these things unconsciously because we are programmed to do so.

1.28 People think in terms of science and religion. They forget the power of economics, The Will to Conform and the power of the herd.

1.28.1 People say religion is the enemy. I'm not so sure. The real enemy is The Will to Conform. Why are people so easily manipulated to follow a religion and not the actual religion, I would think is the real cusp of the problem.

1.29 People are traumatised not because their lives are torn but because they are not living the dream life that they are supposed to live. They expect to be gratified by existence. The simple reality that they are alive is not enough for them. They will only truly value life in the shadow of death.

1.30 People exclaim that they have never been told explicitly that they should conform but this is precisely why the system works. That they are not told or not forced to adopt the system means they placate it more. The best system is one in which the participants refuse to acknowledge it is a system.

1.31 A man does not need a woman and a woman sure as hell doesn't need a man. But are you prepared to counter the power of evolution and education? Are you prepared to flee the herd mentality? Are you prepared to contradict The Will to Conform?

1.32 Existence is not enough. One must have a justified existence. Through conforming one achieves purpose in their life.

1.33 The problem with meeting the constraints of conformity is that it produces anxiety in the individual. The woman with the esteemed career fears the next day at work because she is under pressure. The man who is married must fulfil obligations to keep his marriage intact.

1.34 To be obsessed with what others think of you and to try to gain validation from them is an acceptable form of madness.

1.35 I suspect these notes will not be received positively. The brainwashed of society don't want to be lectured on how hollow life is. They don't want to be schooled on its absurdness. They want to be told that working all your life and marrying are elements worth extoling.

1.36 RD Laing said the cause of schizophrenia was the family nucleus. What one must understand from this is that we are put under severe pressure from friends and family to heed to The Will to Conform. In exchange for individuality we gain acceptance. We unconsciously fear the very people we love.

1.37 Conformity is a form of totalitarianism. Effectively we use men and women as breeding machines to keep an economy alive.

1.38 People are so easily coerced. A good film attacks your unconscious and makes you emotional. That is manipulation. The person you love does the same. Thus, it stands to reason that people are modified or brainwashed into behaving a certain way and wanting certain things and furthermore they are convinced that they consciously make their own decisions. The truth is they are not. They are impelled from a young age to be a certain someone.

1.38.1 The Will to Conform gives not power but the illusion of power. People think they are making their own decisions when they are not. Their choices have been determined since they were children.

1.39 If intelligent life were to pay a visit to earth, what would they see? They would see an animal that has used the tool of language to make great advances. They would see a system that humans use to promote economic growth. They would see that adult men and women are consumed by work and relationships. They would observe in this system that men use women for sexual gratification. They would observe that the female of the species is used as breeding machines to keep the species alive. They would then see that the minds of humans are inflated with romantic jargon pertaining towards love and relationships purely to make the species accept the system and procreate. They would also see the indoctrination of the species when young through systematic education. They would see that this is an animal that in order to feel good is dependent on other animals to endorse them. They would further see that society is addicted to various things such as sex, conversation, image, sports teams, famous people and money and because these addictions are diseases of the majority, they are ascertained to be both normal and acceptable. They would see the power of the herd that labels those who defy the system as outcasts. They would conclude that this species of intelligent animals when living day to day actually doesn't realize who, what and where they are.

1.40 That we are human we reject the concept that we are part of a system. We are so inured on it, so brainwashed that it becomes normality and what one must do in life. The pigs in the abattoir are bred so that they will fuel man's hunger. They are artificially impregnated so that they will rear young. This exact concept applies to men and women. But because we can use language to reason we casually just accept it as the way life works.

1.40.1 What if the system collapsed? Would the resultant society be better off? I doubt it. This is it. The system is the best system we have. A world of anarchy is not better. Your freedom thus is not anarchy but your resilience to rebel. Rebellion in this case is not criminality but the ability to make your own decision on how you should live. People will then retort: "I am making my own choices." Sorry but you are not. Your mind is so warped by The Will to Conform that your choices are predictable and have been made a long time before you decided to choose them. What you will do in life and who you will become has been decided since you were a child.

1.41 There is an anxiety associated with conformity. This conformist anxiety is observed in relationships and careers. A young banker must give a presentation the following day. He becomes anxious and does not get much sleep that night. He fails to realize he is billions of carbon atoms strung together. A middle-aged woman worries that her husband no longer loves her. She becomes stricken with anxiety over her fear of losing him. She fails to realize the enormity of the universe.

1.41.1 I frequently read or hear about people who are unhappy because they see other people who are in relationships and have stellar careers being happy. What does this say? It says that the power of The Will to Conform is casting a shadow over people's lives. It says that people automatically assume that in order to be happy they must be in a relationship and be advancing in their career. Thus, people are not existentially free because their happiness is tied to how they conform.

1.41.2 Case Study: I read of a young woman who had attempted suicide many times and suffers from borderline personality. Her life was in disarray. Fast forward a few years and she now has a boyfriend and job. Prior to this she had said her life was a mess. She wanted to be normal and live a normal life. When she got a boyfriend and job, she finally felt normal. What does this convey? It says that she had come to the conclusion that unless she was working and in a relationship, she couldn't be happy. It says that her existence was not enough. She had to appeal to the eyes of the herd to be happy. She was so polluted by The Will to Conform that simply being alive was not enough. She had to conform to be happy. I see this mentality at work a lot. Men and women yearn to be normal and only through being normal can they be happy. They tie their self-esteem to being endorsed by the herd. They then attribute their failure to be normal to mental illness. They fail to realize that their illness is a product of trying to be normal and not the direct cause of their failure to be normal. They then say in self-pity: "If only I wasn't mentally ill, I could live a normal life," thinking that their illness holds them back. They will continue to live unhappily, and it is only when they are close to death will they appreciate life.

1.41.3 What is the solution? It is simple. Instead of calibrating happiness in terms of relationships, friendships and careers, people begin to cherish their existence. Instead of trying to pacify the herd, they begin to display gratitude for their existence. I feel sorry to an extent for the doctors and psychiatrists who treat these types of people. There is not a lot they can do. There is no pill that can suddenly transform one's life or eradicate anxiety. What the sufferer can do is begin to be so grateful for being alive that they wake up every day in a positive mind frame.

1.41.4 The anxiety ridden individual yearns to be normal. But what is normal in their eyes? It isn't just being alive on this planet. No normal is being in a relationship, succeeding at a career, having adept social skills etc. Think about that for a moment. What it says is that existence does not suffice. We want to live a specific existence and as alluded to this stems from the radicalization of conformity when young.

1.42 Most of us never achieve anything because we measure success in being wanted by the opposite sex. Men want to be wanted by women and women want to be wanted by men. Their whole lives revolve around this conundrum.

1.42.1 We want to be anticipated. That is our strongest want. Thus, men work so that they will become more desirable and women also do the same.

1.42.2 What is attractive for the man is decided by the woman and what is attractive for the woman is decided by the man.

1.42.3 The world is highly dependent on this image obsession to be of value. Men will buy things they do not need to stimulate their image and women also. Existence is not enough. We must be a desired existence.

1.43 A man looks at a woman and determines whether she will improve his image. An attractive woman will also do this. Henceforth therefore men choose the attractive woman. He knows that when he shows her off to friends and family, they will be excited. A woman too thinks of image when she dates a man. She ideally wants a man in high demand because that will astonish her peers.

1.43.1 What it says in effect is that we are under psychological coercion from family and friends. We are always thinking whether a potential partner is deemed worthy because we want to positively influence our family and friends.

1.44 An invisible war wages between what the male of society wants and what the female of society wants, and the outcome is conformity.

1.45 The female of society is under severe obligation from the herd to be a female. She must be the perfect friend, daughter, wife, mother and co-worker.

1.46 If we were born old and never got to experience youth, would we fall in love?

1.47 If you died tomorrow, the world would soldier on. One person is irrelevant to this world. It is only when you add up all the people that you get an economy. People fail to realize this cynical outlook. Life becomes about love and procreation. That we are all worthless is negated. That we will be dead in one hundred years is seldom realized.

Education

2.0 Education is used as a means to proselytize people. Are people naturally moral or does the potential scorn of societies eyes make them moral?

2.1 Is morality congenital or is it learned behaviour? I believe it is the latter.

2.1.1 Through systematic education when young, the minds of society are inculcated to behave a certain way. When young we were taught that subsidizing the herd made us feel content. We carry this mentality into adulthood. When approved by the herd we feel good; when they dismiss us, we feel bad.

2.1.2 Thus people become obsessed with certain things. One of these things is we seek endorsement from the herd as a means to be happy.

2.2 Why when a man or a woman is popular do they feel good? Why when a man is successful does he feel content? Why when a woman is attractive does she feel amorous?

2.3 These things stem from education. Often education and indoctrination are the same thing.

2.3.1 That we are thrown into a snake pit and told to fend for ourselves when young shapes our mentality. Adolescent men learn that having short hair, dressing a particular way and being popular will attract the female's attention. Adolescent women learn that having long hair, dressing a particular way and being attractive will catch the male's attention. This mentality then carries into adulthood and they only grow out of it when they grow old.

2.3.2 From education we are inured on conversation and popularity. That we were thrust into a classroom full of our peers means we must try to survive. Education thus has a huge bearing on why people conform. When we are in the classroom, we begin to realize that we must appease our peers in order to feel good.

2.3.3 We learn that gaining emotional certification from our fellow classmates makes us feel good. Hence, we carry this on into adulthood. What we learned was that when we earned the confirmation of our peers, we felt happy. When they approved of us, we felt good.

2.3.4 Men through being popular gain attention from the females and females by being attractive gain attention from the males. This all occurs in youth during the persuasion of education.

2.4 The one thing education does is that it makes you seek endorsement from the herd.

2.4.1 We then grow up and carry the same methodology into real life. We become obsessed with seeking approbation from our peers. Being wanted makes us feel good and hence why men try to be successful and women try to be attractive, because it makes them feel good about themselves.

2.5 Nobody ever questions the result of being systematically educated. No one ever questions the results of this conformist propaganda.

2.5.1 This is part of the system. It trains people to not question the system. People are so brainwashed that they do not dare attack the mechanism through which they were brainwashed.

2.6 We become addicts of opinion through this indoctrination. We become dependent on admiration from our peers in order to feel good.

2.7 The power of this persuasion cannot be questioned. The religious fundamentalist is brainwashed to commit atrocities. The common man is brainwashed to conform. The world as we accept it is the asylum.

2.7.1 But we do not realize that we are indoctrinated. People thus need protection, not from the world but from themselves.

2.8 Because of education we become obsessed with seeking endorsement from others. We become trained to pour ourselves into corporations to please ourselves. We are instructed to work and slave ourselves. We are schooled to fall in love as a means to live.

2.9 What if we decided to no longer collectively educate our children? What would be the result sociological wise? That we are educated collectively rather than individually has a huge bearing on how we mature as adults

2.10 If we did not systematically educate children, how would they mature as adults? Would they still casually accept the system, or would they be prepared to question it?

2.11 I passionately believe that part of the reason those of Jewish heritage achieve more per population head in life is that they are conditioned to defy The Will to Conform. They are encouraged through their upbringing to think and behave in a unique rather than alike method.

2.12 No one ever ponders the consequence on them as a human being that systematic education has. When one is stressed, they blame the people in their lives. They never acknowledge the influence that education had in shaping their wants and wills.

2.13 Two questions people should ask:

--Why is education mandatory?

--What is the consequence of a mandatory education?

2.14 Because of education we get instructed to think alike rather than critically think as an individual. Education is what is used to change the world and to keep the world from changing.

2.15 Reality is the madness. The means by which we conform is the hallucination. But we are so schooled into seeing normality as just that: normal.

Love

3.0 Love is a form of social control. The 1% who profit in civilization want people to fall in love. Love exists but it is not as common as one thinks. One must differentiate between the system of love that capitalism or life imposes on us (the mythical true love) and Authentic Love.

3.0.1 Authentic love is actual love. It is a profession. It is a discipline. It is a skill one must hone.

3.1 The insanity of our age is this: Believing that one cannot love their existence unless they are loved. This is a sign of immaturity. A mature individual recognises that they must love who they are individually in order to be loved by another.

3.2 Capitalistic love is a very adept system of psychologically incarcerating men and women. That we have had parents indirectly influences us to become them ourselves.

3.2.1 They call it true love to make life more purposeful. What it actually should be called is manipulation. This is especially the case in the capitalistic or narcissistic environment. The man seduces the female through money, ambition, confidence etc. and the female does the same to the man. Just as when you watch a good film or read a good book you become psychologically coerced by that film or book.

3.3 Marriage and relationships are a system of acceptable social control and the result of this system is a contribution to an economy. That is why marriage is extoled.

3.4 Just like a religion has its devoted followers, so too does true love. It is something we have created through language to give intention to life and if we could not speak there would be no such thing as true love, there would only be compassion for each other. It is an ideology like religion.

3.5 If it benefits the system, the model is deemed acceptable. Marriage and relationships benefit the system and thus are glorified. The rules are set up so that economies will thrive.

3.5.1 It is not by law that one must be in a relationship or married. But through proselytization when young we come to adopt the system as final.

3.5.2 Authentic love is a profession that needs dedication and perseverance. In order to engage in Authentic Love, one must be mature. To be mature, one must not be narcissistic.

3.5.3 I believe in sexual attraction; I believe in the power of the herd and image; I believe in the pressure that society is under; I believe in the compulsion to avoid boredom; I believe in our ability to speak. When you combine all these qualities the result is the system of true love and that is what it is, a system.

3.6 We are just animals. Our bodies are atoms; our minds are neurons. We afford existence more than what is worth. That we can reason with ourselves through language, we make ourselves out to be special. We are all the same.

3.7 The sole purpose is to contribute to an economy. But people do not like this thought. They want to have purpose in their life. This is why we have given birth to this "true love" system, wherein people are told to fall in love and procreate. Now this is an ambition which they actually can tolerate. Thus, we are told to fall in love and raise a family purely to contribute to an economy. True love is a romanticized ideology. It is a means of controlling society so that they will subsidize an economy. The real enemy is not terrorists or religions or science, the real enemy is The Will to Conform, the real enemy is economics.

3.7.1 One must distinguish between true love the fantasy and Authentic Love the skill. This idea that there is one person in the world you are meant to be with is fantasy. There are many people you can actually love.

3.7.2 When love is done right, as in Authentic Love, it is what makes life worth it. Unfortunately, modern day capitalism as contaminated love.

3.8 Both men and women are threatening to negatively label each other with regards sex. Men can be labelled "perverts" by women and women can be slut shamed by men. The consequence of these threats is that people are funnelled towards a relationship in order to have sex. A huge part of the popularity of love is that it is not stigmatized. (I go into this in more detail in later notes such as The Labelling Phenomenon: Volume Two.)

3.8.1 Now the world economies are dependent on it. The 1% who really gain need the 99% to follow the model. They need people to marry and raise families. Capitalism is in part dependent on the family nucleus to function. The puppeteers are dependent on their puppets. This has stemmed from education. Through education we are put in a room with other children and as such we learn to want their endorsement. When we grow up, we simply carry this temperament into the real world.

3.9 People are effectively conned by this economic necessity disguised as true love.

3.10 With relationships in the modern capitalistic environment, we essentially tell men and women that they cannot be happy alone.

3.11 Love in part stems from the existential anxiety. We do not want to live in a world of absurdness, so we suppress these reptilian thoughts through adopting the system of love-conquers-all.

3.12 People do not realize just how easily they are manipulated. They are programmed to believe in god and in true love, just like we program a computer to work. One can see this at play. Go around to schools and you will see this behaviour wherein adolescents become engrossed in making others happy to make themselves happy. They become absorbed in relationships and careers. They become brainwashed. But because it is both acceptable and a necessity for economies, we say it is rational behaviour.

3.12.1. There is authentic love, which is something I believe in and which is also extremely rare. This is the kind of love between two people who have nothing except themselves. Then there is this other manifestation of capitalistic love that is a combination of confidence, money, background, looks, education and intelligence of which the individual(s) exclaim it is true love when it is not.

3.13 Women do possess power. The law-abiding society you live in is a product of the herd and the herd consists of men and women. Both men and women interpret each other. Both want to be labelled positively by each other. If men are deviant with regards sex, they get labelled negatively, such as being called a "pervert." This then makes men, those that are moral, gravitate towards relationships.

3.14 We always try to roll the dice in our favour. We always try to justify our beliefs.

3.15 A question people should ask is: "Why when I get flattered sexually do I feel good?" Why does a man feel good when he is wanted by a female? Why does a woman feel good when she is wanted by a man?

3.15.1 The reason is because from education they have become accustomed to feel good when validated by the herd. When we were adolescents it was the popular male and the good-looking female that gained positive validation. We carry this immature attitude into adulthood.

3.16 The feelings one experiences for someone they "love" are the exact same feelings one feels when they watch a good movie or read a good book. One is psychologically manoeuvred to feel that way. The book, the film and the relationship are exploiting your mind. As Erich Fromm remarked, feelings are temporary; they dissipate with time and as such authentic love is more than a feeling.

3.17 In marriage men and women both possess power and lack it. In gaining power over each other they lose their own autonomy. The question is: Is it better to own yourself or to own another? This is the price of a relationship. You lose your own control but gain another's.

3.18 We effectively deprive ourselves of freedom when we enter into a relationship. Conformity thus is not the best system in my opinion because one is dependent on another person for their completeness. One must begin to realize that the simplest life is solitude. If one can find solace in the loneliness, they will discover a happiness that cannot be taken from them.

3.18.1 One must begin to understand this pattern. Men and women reject themselves as individually viable to be happy. They say to themselves: "I can't be happy until I am in love." This is a narcissistic approach.

3.19 Just as a film makes one feel good so does another person. So, a man sees a woman who is attractive and speaks well and comes from a good background.

3.20 Honest or authentic love is extremely rare. Just as one can only be free in solitude, those in love must love each other in their own solitude. How many marry to placate the herd? How many marry to enhance their image? How many marry to succumb to evolutionary instinct? How many marry for financial motives? The mark of honest love is if you took away all the sociological privileges that marriage provides and the two souls are left naked with nothing but each other, would their love still burn bright in this dying dark universe?

3.21 One thing that disappoints me about the existential writers is that they promote love and its system as a means to be happy. They never look at the pattern of love the social engineered fantasy that dominates society in economic terms.

3.22 People are like drug addicts in a sense. They require an emotional response from life itself. Typically, this comes from vindication and validation from other people. They become dependent on the herd to be happy.

3.23 The best system is one in which the participants do not realize it is a system. This is what modern day conformity does. People are in complete denial that they have been emotionally exploited. Think about it. Nearly eight billion people all behave the same way and want the same things. There is something at work, ergo The Will to Conform.

3.24 A relationship may make you content, but it may not. The simplest system is to become one with the universe, as in to be grateful for just being alive. But we are so afraid of the herd and its judgment that we are unconsciously provoked into doing what the herd wants us to do.

3.25 An insecure woman says: My boyfriend makes me feel loved. What does this mean? It means that in order for her to be befitting of her existence she needs external love. It says she cannot be happy in this universe until she is loved. This is replicated across billions of people on this planet we call earth. Humans say they cannot love their existence until they are loved by another. It is immature, if not insane to have such a mentality.

3.26 Without language there is no such thing as true love. There is only pure naked compassion. True love like religion is a system we have concocted to provide meaning because we can speak.

3.27 The animal must worry about food, shelter and predators. Man worries about whether he is liked. The system of economies dominates mankind whereas a system of survival dominates animals.

3.28 We are animals. Do lions or cattle have "soul mates?"

3.29 Love becomes a form of psychological dependence. It becomes an escape. It becomes an addiction. I believe it is a means to forget oneself in this indifferent universe.

3.30 The great deception or illusion is that you are making your own choices by your own conscious input. You are not. What you will do with your life, what you will become has been decided the moment you are indoctrinated through education. Your liberty, if anything, is to defy how your unconscious has been programmed.

3.31 One does not need another person to be complete. They do not need to fall in love to be fully human. They can love and cherish their own existence. They can be happy in the solitude. This is ironically the starting point for Authentic Love. The people can thrive in Authentic Love are the ones who are not infatuated with love.

3.32 Relationships become commoditized. By this I mean that the symbol of the relationship is treated as an object for the male or female to gain respect from his or her peers.

3.31 I cannot emphasize it enough. About 40% of the reason we wish to be in a relationship is to manage our presentation to society. We wish to avoid being stigmatized.

3.32 Both the male and female want to be overwhelmed by potential partners. The man thus goes for the attractive woman because that captivates him. The woman goes for the in-demand guy because that mesmerizes her.

3.33 The acid test of any relationship is that if they lost everything, their house, their business and their money, except each other, would the love survive? Very few would because they are using their relationship to further their image to the world. This is the consumerism of love.

Gratification

4.0 We are bored and wait for life to gratify us. We take our existence for granted and don't fathom how fortunate we are to be alive.

4.1 We are soldiers of gratification. We use relationships, friendships, careers, films, sports teams, etc. to fuel our happiness. Buddhism teaches that all one needs to be happy is to exist. It is a matter of reprogramming your unconscious mind to be indebted for being alive.

4.2 The mechanics of a date, watching a sports match or reading a book are all the same. We must be entertained by them to feel glad. When we are not beguiled by them, we generally reject them and go elsewhere to find solace.

4.2.1 Everything in life is thus an opportunity to escape life. A relationship, a book, a film, a conversation, a friend etc. are all means to escape unto life.

4.2.2 The individual does not realize that they use a trip to the pub or a sports team as a means to quash the boredom. The activity must make you feel good or else that escape has failed.

4.3 Anticipation of the event is often greater than the event. Often the hype before the event is better than the actual event. In this case we are not gratified.

4.4 If the event is boring it will not entertain. Conversely if the event is too entertaining it will not entertain either. There is a balance to be found.

4.4.1 Entertainment thus lies somewhere in between.

4.5 We are sexual addicts. Furthermore, we teach the next generation that it is wrong to be asexual. This is done so that they will be pressured into wanting to have sex or form a relationship.

4.6 Life is thus a choice between boredom and gratification (entertainment) and the choice of gratification carries the threat of encountering suffering.

4.7 Conversation for instance must entertain. We generally like to listen to those who converse well, and we dismiss those who do not speak well.

4.7.1 We use conversation as a gauge to judge people. We align ourselves to those who speak confidently and demean those who mumble.

4.8 It is in our quest to be gratified that we suffer. If only we could accept our boredom a little bit better. Boredom is the true enemy.

4.9 We use each other as escapes. You use your partner just like a film to escape life and enjoy yourself.

4.9.1 We use people as an avenue of escape. We use a relationship or a friendship to allow us to pass the time and to feel enlivened.

4.9.2 We must beguile others. This demand is unconscious or else they fall out with us. Every interaction involves a game. From youth we are programmed to respond unconsciously to other human beings.

4.9.3 We must please each other. We must appropriately respond to each other. When someone inappropriately responds to another, friction is created.

4.10 We expect to be stimulated by everyone. Life is so great that we are condemned to flee it every second of every day.

4.11 Buddhism teaches that man must become more tolerable of his boredom to relax in life. It preaches the art of meditation as a means to become one with nature.

4.11.1 Instead of expecting the world to emotionally subsidize man, man finds comfort in the solitude and through doing this, he sets himself free.

4.12 We are drug addicts of existence. Life is a drug that must keep on delivering. When it delivers, we feel content. But when we are deprived of this drug, we feel anxious.

4.12.1 People thus become hooked on other people as a means to achieve happiness in this world. Our partner becomes a source of our euphoria and should they abandon us we feel the same way as if we were deprived of our narcotic drug.

4.12.2 Now this is dangerous because it means we leverage our happiness on another person. We mortgage our futures on a happy marriage. But people by default are unpredictable and irrational. They do not always do what we wish them to do.

4.13 A relationship is the simplest form of happiness from the viewpoint of the herd. But in terms of the individual it is not the most elementary form. The most basic form of happiness with regards the individual is solitude.

4.14 If you can make yourself happy in solitude, you will possess a happiness that cannot be taken from you.

4.14.1 But the world lives in fear of the herd. They live in fear of the very people they love and this strives to induce the system of marriage within them.

Interpretation

5.0 Every interaction between two or more people involves acceptance and rejecting. We either accept what they say or do or we reject it. We either agree with each other or we disagree. So, if we are talking to another person and that person suddenly hits us on the face, we reject that interaction.

5.0.1 Every event (action, word spoken) is either: accepted, rejected or ignored by us. Everything is either: accepted or rejected; appropriate or inappropriate; impressive or unimpressive. Everything is interpretation and interpretation is everything.

5.0.2 A disagreement is simply an action or conversation that is rejected.

5.1 Acceptance is often done unconsciously. Someone stops to chat, and we accept what they do and what they say. The majority of acceptance is unconscious. Someone may say something to which the observer responds on instinct.

5.1.1 If that someone said something unusual or attacked us, we would reject that action.

5.1.2 We accept without realizing it. Generally, rejection permeates to the conscious. We become consciously aware that someone has done something wrong.

5.2 At the heart of it all we want to be labelled fittingly in life.

5.2.1 All our fears lie in being interpreted negatively. A woman who deems herself unattractive does so from the point of the viewing herd. That the herd will label her unattractive causes her to feel disconsolate. The same applies to the male of society. Thus, what we chase in life is not success but rather the positive labels that success endeavours to produce. We do so because when we are labelled positively, we feel good. This reliance on positive labels is formulated in childhood through education.

5.3 Whence you encounter another individual you become interpreted by that individual. In being interpreted you become labelled and in being labelled you become condemned.

5.4 Interpretation plus language gives right or wrong. We construct the law to suit the needs of the majority. Crime is but a matter of interpretation.

5.5 The price one must pay for being accepted by friends or a partner is that we expose ourselves to potential rejection from these very entities. This ultimately is the risk of being recognised by society. Interpretation often leads to despair.

5.6 Groups tend to follow a similar mechanism with regards labelling. Initially we get introduced to the group and all is well. People mingle and enjoy each other's company. Gradually people get to know each other more and start to label others. Eventually two or more people group together and segregate another person or persons. This happens in all groups. People become segregated and labelled by other people in the group.

5.7 As long as two people interact, they will interpret each other and thus there can be a breakdown in acceptance.

5.7.1 The more you associate yourself with the herd, the more you will be ushered to adopt their mantra unconsciously over fear of reprisals.

5.8 We take this acceptance of others on us for granted. We do not realize that once we immerse ourselves in others and become known by them, we are forever subject to their interpretation of us. A failed marriage or a failed friendship in this case is just a negative opinion by others on us.

5.9 In some cases the same action can either be accepted or rejected depending on the interpretation of this receiver. As in one individual can accept the event but a different individual can reject that same event. This creates an argument or debate within society.

5.9.1 This is known as The Rashomon Effect: Identical events can be interpreted differently by different people.

5.9.2 Furthermore the interpretation of the individual can change over time. One may interpret something positively now, but in ten years' time they may interpret the same thing negatively.

5.9.3 This is what complicates life because two people can have different interpretations of the same event.

5.10 We decide what is right and wrong to suit our needs. We say a terrorist that kills on the streets of Paris is wrong, but the government that bombs a remote village in the Middle East is right.

5.11 We pick and choose when things are acceptable and when they are not. It is all right to dress in swimming attire when going to the swimming pool. But one cannot wear swimming attire in the office. The office will reject it. We take what we accept for granted as we could easily live in a world where love was a crime and conversation was a death sentence.

5.12 It just so happens that relationships are extoled in this world. We could easily live in a world wherein they were illegal. There is no right nor wrong only our interpretation of right or wrong.

5.13 Interpretation coupled with language decides the law. Interpretation is ninety percent of life.

5.13.1 There will always be disagreements in life between two or more people because people unconsciously analyse the behaviour. The action is either acceptable/impressive/appropriate or it is unacceptable/not impressive/inappropriate. Thus, as long as we live in a socialized world, people will have disagreements. The only way you get rid of crime is if you change the law or if everyone avoids everyone. Take a car accident. A car (Car A) crashes into the back of another car (Car B). The driver of (Car A) says immediately, that is inappropriate. A disagreement occurs. Now apply this to every other disagreement in life.

5.13.2 Thus dealing with people carries the threat of a negative reaction both by us on them and by them on us. It is a psychological minefield.

5.14 From this we produce the victim/perpetrator mechanism. One person gets labelled the perpetrator and the recipient is labelled the victim.

5.15 The subject of interpretation is special to humans. With animals it is friend/food/foe. With humans it is more ambiguous. A gazelle will always fear a lion. That is its interpretation. With humans it is not so simple. We glamourize the genius of society; we shame the criminals. We like some people and fear others.

5.15.1 The geniuses and the monsters are distinguished only by interpretation.

5.16 Our minds thus are warped by the presence of those who know us. When we become known by another person, we become labelled by them and once we are labelled, we are condemned.

5.16.1 To be known is to be condemned and to be condemned is to be known. Just as a parent star warps the fabric of space time around a planet, people are distorted by the presence of those that know them. Thus, they live to pacify the will of others. They live to earn validation from others.

5.16.2 Either way people are labelled. The criminal is criminal; the social recluse who tries to live a simple life is called odd.

5.17 We take our acceptance for granted. We can so easily be rejected should we stray from the herd. As such we chase the positive labels and try to avoid the negative labels.

5.18 We have systems of acceptable and unacceptable. How do we define good and bad? What we do is be adopt certain systems. By this I mean the herd adopts certain methodologies for how events must occur. If an action occurs that takes place outside this circle of acceptable behaviour, we label it negatively.

5.18.1 We have models on what is acceptable, on what is ignored and on what is unacceptable. Now are these things in the grander scheme of things within this universe right or wrong? No. We are simply animals who have concocted laws to maximise the potential of the system, the system being a flourishing economy.

5.19 Is the behaviour deviant or is it one's interpretation of the behaviour that makes it deviant? We will always have crime because of this, because we interpret everything.

5.19.1 Thus if one truly wishes to be free, they would be advised to live in solitude. In solitude you cannot be attacked by the opinion of others.

5.20 We are at the mercy of another person's interpretation of us. That they can label us fills us with dread. Our lives thus centre around obtaining a positive label from another person.

5.21 We engage in Interpretation Game Theory.

--Does that person like me?

--How does that person see me?

5.22 Fame thus is a slow form of suicide. To be known by your peers induces tension within; to be known by the whole world means that they will label you as you walk down the street.

5.23 There is no right and wrong in this world, but the system is extoled and anything that deviates from the system is labelled accordingly.

5.24 Through The Will to Conform we decide what is acceptable and unacceptable. People then unconsciously buy into this ideal.

5.24.1 We pick and choose when things are acceptable and unacceptable. There is no right or wrong, but we decide what is beneficial to us and what isn't. The rules we possess are just things we as humans have realized to make economies thrive.

5.24.2 The law is as wrong as it is right; it is as correct as it is incorrect. The law is just a means to channel society into contributing to economies. This system of reimbursing economies is the system we have chosen. It could easily be a different system such as war.

5.25 We are all insane and sane. It is just a matter of perspective. We are all mad, but what the herd does is considered normality. Madness is relative.

5.26 The court is just a system to maintain a prosperous economy. There are no rules. Everything is permitted. In a parallel universe love is a crime. It is all crime. Existence is a crime, we just decide when it is lawful or not.

5.27 What one must understand is that normality is the insanity. People falling in love and working is madness but because everyone does it and because it is extoled by the majority, it becomes accepted as normal. Reality is the hallucination. Normality is an acceptable form of psychosis.

5.29 That our full identity is not known in internet forums means we are liable to say things we normally wouldn't. Thus, people are more prone to saying stupid things or getting into arguments. They do so because their identity is not fully known. They wear a mask of sorts and this allows them to behave differently.

5.30 The most futile thing in the world is arguing over one's interpretation. Arguments can never be right, only more convenient. We unconsciously expect that people will see rational and when they don't, we become frustrated.

Labels

6.0 The price one must pay for living is that we become labelled.

6.0.1 When you become known, you become labelled and thus try to be emotionally vindicated by the person who knows you. You become caged by their opinion of you. You misplace your freedom and commit existential suicide.

6.0.2 When you know someone and they know you, you are put under pressure by them. Now apply this logic to family and friends. They put us under duress to behave a certain way.

6.1 Existential suicide: We label the criminal. He is forever condemned. What the law-abiding citizens fail to realize is that they too are condemned, once they are known. Just as the planet is locked in orbit by the parent star, man too is held in orbit by the eyes of society. He unconsciously becomes afraid to violate the herd. He fears his very friends, family and peers. Man is terrified to be an individual.

6.2 One cannot be labelled "nothing." One is always labelled. If they exist, they will be labelled. When you know someone, you label them. The known man is condemned to be labelled. The more you know someone the more you risk labelling them. Once known, man is assaulted by labels and by society's analysis of him.

6.3 The law-abiding citizen automatically pursues desirable labels. Hence, they hunt success and relationships so that they can be labelled positively. What if they become negatively labelled? They feel bad. Thus, our mental wellbeing is connected to labels.

6.4 We tie our self-esteem to being approbated by another human. We basically say that we cannot be happy unless another person is happy for us.

6.4.1 We live to be emotionally vindicated by society. In doing so we are labelled positively and thus feel good. Thus, a man chases an appropriate label, as does the woman. Thus, your freedom if anything is to escape this tyranny and not be impinged by the eyes of others. Life would be so much simpler if we were all blind. The very organ that gives us the ability to perceive the world is the same organ that restricts our individuality.

6.5 Albert Einstein said that matter warps the space time fabric. Thus, a parent star warps this fabric so much that it pushes against a planet and the planet becomes locked in orbit. This is what being known by another person does to us. They distort our presence and behaviour. We adapt to placate their opinions; we become a prisoner to their interpretation of us and vice versa. The mentally healthy person does not realize this. They waltz through life meeting people, unaware of the fact that they are being moulded to behave a certain way by the very people they depend on.

6.5.1 We are psychologically warped by the presence of those who know us. Those who know us mould us. They influence our response to life. We unconsciously live in fear of a negative opinion by them on us. This is the Labelling Anxiety that shadows the life of man. You cannot see it but only feel it. Just as matter warps the fabric of space time; man is warped by the presence of those who know him.

6.5.2 When you enter a room full of people and socialize with them, you become warped by their presence in knowing you. You control their behaviour and they control yours. You seek verification from them and they from you. You categorize them and they categorize you. Thus, the herd controls the behaviour of the individual and the individual controls the behaviour of the herd. With schizophrenia this mechanism is defective. The schizophrenic does not wish to be controlled by another individual or the herd.

6.5.3 To be known by a fellow human being means one will be psychologically bent to the will of that person. This force is unconscious. One does not realize that they are being put under psychological duress to behave a certain way. This applies to family and friends (peers). They put one under so much burden to be a certain someone. Men must behave a certain way as must women.

6.5.4 For example take a person who becomes famous. Before their fame they were unknown. They were able to walk down the street and nobody cared about them. Then when they became famous, they became known and to become known means they are positively labelled. But a positive label is actually a means by which society controls society. Let me explain why in the case of this famous person. They now (post fame) must conduct themselves in such a fashion that they placate the world. They must be careful what they say and what they do. They must meet the constraints of conformity or else the public will not respect them. Now apply this mentality to the ordinary individual. Those who know him including his loved family and friends actually sculpt his existence. Thus, it stands to reason that the only way one can truly be free is to live in solitude.

6.5.5 This is why fame is as much a nightmare as much as it is a bonus. Your peers will label you. Now imagine that your peers were the whole world. Imagine walking down the street and everyone recognises you and with recognition comes a label. There can be no freedom with such a life. For example, a famous person who is HIV+ is labelled HIV+ by the world. But what if this famous person wasn't famous? What if he was just an ordinary man? Only his doctor and perhaps family would be aware of his diagnosis. Only they would label him. But because he is world famous, he becomes labelled and with the label comes the stigma.

6.5.6 You often read of those famous people who attest that fame ruined their lives. They talk about the burden and pressure they were put under to conform. What one must do is apply this same mentality to the individual who is not famous. To be known through the eyes of the common man is a subdued form of fame but the same rules still apply. Just as the famous person is under pressure from society to behave a certain way, so too is the non-famous individual that is known by his peers. Thus, as I say repeatedly throughout these notes, if you want to be free, truly free, live in solitude.

6.6 We instinctively chase appropriate labels in life because we feel good when we are labelled fittingly. The successful man gets labelled positively by the female; the attractive female gets labelled positively by the male. Furthermore, we chase the labels that are symbolic of happiness (careers and relationships) because when the herd acknowledges us under these labels, they approve of us. The problem is that the labels of happiness do not necessary equate to happiness. Just because you have the relationship and career does not mean you are happy. You may look happy but may not actually be happy.

6.6.1 Are you happy or are you just pretending to be happy?

6.7 Rudyard Kipling said that the greatest luxury in life was in owning yourself. That is your existential freedom. To not be held ransom by another person. With relationships you may gain acceptance from the herd (parents, friends, peerage) but you lose your own autonomy. For you to make the relationship survive you must compromise in some way.

6.8 The herd motivates and warps the individual's behaviour. This applies to family, friends and co-workers. They put the individual under severe hardship to behave a certain way. When the individual loses confirmation, he feels discontent.

6.9 Stigma is just labels. People possess an unconscious fear of being stigmatized.

6.10 The mentally sound individual does not feel the effects of being labelled. They are used to it. But should they make a mistake or error and become negatively labelled, they then feel its effects. Labelling however is the fulcrum of schizophrenia. They fear being labelled or being known.

6.11 On social media for instance people post pictures which they know will generate a positive reprisal from the viewing herd. They deliberately always try to induce endorsement from the herd.

6.12 Now this control or labelling anxiety stems from language. That we can speak means we can label and that we can label means we can control society.

6.13 The common person who is psychologically healthy does not realize the consequences of being known. They automatically think that the criminal is negatively labelled and is vilified by society. They do not realize the negative aspect of being positively labelled. One sells their freedom when they become known. One cannot be labelled if they are not known but one is labelled even if they are accepted by society. Thus, there is no such thing as a positive label. A positive label is in fact always a negative label. One can only be free when they are unknown.

6.13.1 A positive label is in a sense a negative label because the individual must first compromise to obtain the positive label and secondly must accede further to maintain the positive label.

6.14 Case Study: John is a common working and married man. He tries to be successful and look nice. In doing so he becomes positively labelled by society. He has a wife that loves him and a comfortable job that rewards him. Both serve to psychologically endorse him and he feels good about such an arrangement. Thus, it stands to reason from this arrangement in life we don't chase happiness; we chase the labels that label us happy. A man wants to be labelled successful and rich because this is what procures positive labels from society. A woman wants to be labelled attractive because this is what procures positive labels from her peers. They tie their self-esteem to being labelled positively by the herd. Thus, they are not free. They are imprisoned by the eyes of the herd. It is the majority who dictates how they conduct themselves and not their own conscious decision. Thus, a positive label is in fact a source of tyranny. In chasing a positive label, we lose our freedom because we are trying to appease the herd.

6.15 People automatically deduce that freedom is not being in jail. This is part of the brainwashing. People do not realize that the criminals have more liberty than the common man who is a slave to opinion and money. The criminal is enclosed by concrete walls; the free man is enslaved by the herd's interpretation of him. Labelling is a form of social control.

6.16 The less people know of you, the more liberty you possess.

6.16.1 Imagine two people Person A (PA) and Person B (PB). They both know each other. Thus, they are both under pressure to validate each other. They both must submit to the other person to be circumstantiated. They both control each other's behaviour. Now take for instance they are walking towards each other and (PA) says hello to (PB), but (PB) just ignores (PA). (PA) now thinks that was rude. They thus fall out and no longer approve each other. Now apply this to more than two people in a workplace or school. You control your friends and they control you.

6.16.2 So what people do is this. They try to obtain positive labels from the herd. Thus, a husband tries to conciliate his wife and the wife tries to conciliate her husband. However, they fail to realize that they both must compromise their behaviour in order to come to a positive agreement. They both are warped by each other. Thus, it stands to reason that if you don't know anyone you won't be compromised in any way or form.

6.16.3 It is better to be nothing than it is to be known. You have far more freedom being anonymous than you do in being recognised.

6.17 That we are labelled or could be potentially labelled, represses us. Thus, we conform implicitly and deny our true calling. The common man does not see this invisible pressure of labels on him. It is only when he falls out with family, friends or co-workers does he realize its power.

6.17.1 We are caught in a bind. Society says one must bathe themselves in other people. But in immersing ourselves in other people carries the threat of being labelled negatively by society itself. The price one must pay to involve themselves in life is that they may become labelled and once they are labelled, they are condemned.

6.18 The fear that haunts Kafka in The Trial is the terror of being known. That the protagonist is arrested and paraded before society amounts to a psychological rape of his identity.

6.19 The wild animal when faced with a predator becomes anxious. Man, when faced with becoming labelled becomes nervous. The animals must worry about food, shelter and predators; man, only worries about his reputation. The animal fears the teeth of the predator; man fears the jaws of being labelled.

6.19.1 Man is the only animal that can sin. When an animal kills an animal, it is called nature. When man kills an animal, it is grotesque. We unconsciously believe that men because they have the tool of language should be moral.

6.20 We affiliate ourselves with entities that make us feel good. It's how famous people and sports teams make their money.

6.21 We label those who do not contribute to the economy. The mentally ill, the sick and the old all get labelled accordingly. Thus, it can be postulated that the sole purpose of labels is to channel society into contributing to an economy. The fear of a negative label keeps a man moral. The apprehension of being labelled negatively pressurizes him to obtain positive labels. The herd makes him conform purely so that he will subsidize an economy. On an individual level labelling makes a man conform; on a macro level it is the fuel of economies.

6.22 It is in doing in life that we become undone. It is in chasing gratification that we make mistakes. A mistake is a negative label in the eyes of another individual. In our quest to feel pleasure we become damned.

6.23 A lot of people's anxiety is over their failure to be normal. This is the power of The Will to Conform. It harbours an anxiety in those who do not meet the standard of the herd. Although the individual may not be criminal, that they are not labelled positively by the herd causes them distress. That the individual fails to meet the criteria of The Will to Conform causes them to become angst ridden. This is down to the Labelling Anxiety that can shadow the lives of so many.

6.24 We cherish the individual's positive opinion of us but we also unconsciously fear this opinion of us.

6.25 Just as one chases designer clothing or a particular brand of car to entice their peers, they chase the labels of conformity (marriage; esteemed job) so they will appeal to the herd. They chase the labels that make them look privileged. That is the power of The Will to Conform.

6.25.1 To the healthy individual this Labelling Anxiety is minute and not noticeable unless they commit a crime etc. To the neurotic this labelling anxiety is profound. They fear being negatively labelled by the herd.

6.26 Everyone we meet, we play an invisible form of game theory with them.

--If I do this, how will they react?

6.26.1 Thus this game theory keeps us lawful. We are afraid of other people's opinions so much that we seek to uphold them at all costs.

6.27 We wish to react otherwise but in doing so we know we will gain a negative opinion. To be known is actually what we fear. To be known is the crime; opinion is the punishment.

6.27.1 We conform to be liked and that makes us feel good. We want to feel good. We are slaves to our emotion. Our soul is exhausted in seeking endorsement.

6.27.2 Furthermore we expect to be entertained by people. On one hand we fear people; on the other hand, we wish them to enthral us.

6.28 Life is toxic. All our stresses are in some way connected to people. We unconsciously fear their labels. And yet we do not flee them. Language has created this huge schism in the minds of men. Through systematic education they need the nourishment of conversation, but the hearts of men are filled with such poison. People do not realize that the very thing they yearn for is actually killing them.

6.29 Man is every label that is available. When he acts, he then becomes labelled. He has the potential to be labelled under every banner. All he must do is live and through living he makes mistakes.

6.30 No label is better than a positive label. We all are just a label away from being criminal.

6.30.1 Man by himself and alone is nothing. It is only when he encounters another man that he becomes labelled. He is nothing and then he crystalizes into something.

6.30.2 All our woes lie in being known. All our stresses lie in some way or form with people. The less people know of you, the less they can label you. If you do not know someone you cannot label them. There is a comfort in being anonymous.

One is condemned when one is known. One cannot fight or flee a label.

6.30.3 People cannot comprehend this. They complain about their lives not being good and yet they are blind to the reality that their life is being made troublesome by other people. Furthermore, they think that the solution lies in other people. A lot of this stress lies in being labelled.

6.31 The minute we walk into a room full of people we are labelled. One cannot be known and not be labelled. The mistake is not in being labelled but in being known in the first place. They cannot label you if they do not recognise you.

6.32 We mortgage our self-esteem on endorsement (friends; family), image and being in a relationship. One should just be content to be alive in this universe.

6.33 We are dealing with unpredictable and irrational people and yet we tie our futures to them. One has better luck at the roulette table.

6.34 People get lectured what dreams they should have. Men and women have resolved to marry thirty years before they get married. Their lives are calculated. They are drip fed their futures.

6.35 Relationships become the means by which a man is measured. And many people are led to find love because of the fear of others and not by their own conscious choice.

6.36 The cusp of the problem is that man computes his self-worth in the two-dimensional aspects of relationships and careers. But in his failure to meet the stipulations of this methodology of living he becomes negatively labelled. Your freedom if anything is your ability to overcome this anxiety; to not live in fear of the herd.

6.37 Our greatest hopes and worst fears lie in being recognised.

6.37.1 Imagine for instance a married husband and wife. The husband cheats on his wife. The wife then formulates a negative opinion of the husband. The husband consequently feels dejected in himself. Now what if he had never married in the first place? What if he had never known his wife or any woman for that matter? He would not have gotten into trouble and thus wouldn't feel dejected over the negative opinion on him because there is no opinion at all. You see our daily lives are spent in a battle trying to gain or maintain a positive image from our peerage. People don't see the battle, but it exists, characterizing their existence like gravity.

6.38 The goal of existential nihilistic therapy is to rid man of this Labelling Anxiety. This can be achieved through making him aware of the realities of this universe. That man is insignificant can set him free. When he realizes that he is trillions of carbon atoms stuck together; when he realizes the scope of the universe above and below him; when he realizes that he is just an animal with the tool of language he may just rid himself of his fear of being labelled. In dissolving his Labelling Anxiety, he no longer approaches life in a state of anxiety. He comes to value how lucky he is to be alive. He thus becomes grateful for being alive.

6.39 To be known is like a virus. Your identity becomes distributed by society. People will attack and demean your identity. Labels must be thought of as a virus that spread from host to host. When you become known by a certain person, they transfer their knowledge of you to another person.

6.40 To be known is to be condemned and to be condemned is to be known. All anxieties lie in the eyes of others. We fear opinion not fists.

6.41 If you wish to liberate man, educate him individually and not collectively.

Conformist Anxiety

7.0 Conformism produces an anxiety in people. Their failure to conform results in them becoming anxious because they have failed to find a suitable career or a suitable partner.

7.0.1 Some of the anxiety we call mental illness is anxiety over the failure to meet the stipulations of conformity. It is one's failure to be normal. Their failure to be in a relationship or to have a productive career causes the individual to feel depressed.

7.0.2 Some of the mentally ill suffer angst over their failure to meet the stipulations of The Will to Conform. So many are distraught over their failure to be mediocre.

7.0.3 People automatically measure their worth in terms of relationships and careers. When they falter at these things so too does their optimism for life. They must be chewed out of this implicit Will to Conform.

7.1 I notice that those stricken with anxiety often attest that if they were not ill, their lives would be better. What they fail to realize is that their anxiety is a derivative of life and not independent of life itself.

7.1.1 What I mean by this is that their anxiety is a direct consequence of interacting with the world. It is not some independent disease that afflicts them. Basically, if the sufferer does not absorb themselves in the world, they won't feel anxious. But so many are damned through the power of The Will to Conform, that any other system is rejected.

7.1.2 The world is not in the wrong; it is how one interacts with the world that is wrong. One must conclude that they cannot function to the appropriate standard in the world. They are defective psychologically and through this acceptance they concentrate on what they can do effectively

7.1.3 This anxiety associated with one's failure to conform is not independent of environment; it is a reaction to environment. People will automatically deduce that if they weren't psychiatrically ill their existence would be better. But they cannot say this because their psychiatric illness (anxiety) is a response to the very world they live in. No world equals no anxiety.

7.1.4 They have been so polluted with the power of The Will to Conform that they can only measure success in terms of relationships and careers. The power of the herd casts a dark shadow over their life. The very fact that those who fail to conform feel anxious demonstrates just how brainwashed they are to conform. They observe other people who are "succeeding" in life and they yearn for the same.

7.2 I read of so many people who say they have anxiety for their perceived failure at life. They blame their inability to get a partner or do well in their job on their mental illness. In particular they attest that their anxiety restrains them sociologically. I am sorry to say but I don't think it is mental illness that holds them back. They simply lack the ability to do well in these areas. Psychiatric illnesses that inhibit people are Schizophrenia or Bipolar. They actually interfere with someone's ability to perform at a certain level. If you have severe anxiety with regards a relationship or a job, this is your mind telling you that it doesn't want to do this thing. It simply is the inability to perform in that environment. The mind of this person simply does not have the mechanism to cope.

7.2.1 But it can cope in another environment. The problem is that people with anxiety are in a bind socially. Society dictates that in order to be understood as respectable, individuals must work in good jobs and must be in relationships. But the mind of these individuals wants to do otherwise. They then latch onto this anxiety wildcard to justify their failings, when the real reason is that they simply do not have the psychological ability to perform in this environment. If someone were fully deaf, they would not be expected to work in certain environments. The same applies to those who experience terrible anxiety. They cannot be expected to function in jobs or relationships or both perhaps.

7.3 We have an idea of how our lives should be. When the criteria is not met we tend to become distressed.

7.4 This conformist anxiety is a plague on the western man. He forgets he is an animal. He forgets the tragic universe. But most of all he forgets how lucky he is to be alive.

7.5 What happens when the dream life becomes a nightmare that we cannot bear? What happens when we cannot psychologically handle The Will to Conform? We try and try and keep doing the same thing twenty times expecting different results. The Will to Conform is a system that does not benefit everyone. Not everyone gains from it. But you can find a system that you can achieve from.

7.5.1 One must embrace who they are. People suffer over their failure to be normal.

7.6 Accepting defeat can galvanise you. When you come to realize that you can't do this and that, you can start looking at what you can do. People may say their psychiatric illness holds them back. It doesn't. Their own perception holds them back. As Laing said mental illness can be a breakdown or a break-through. It all depends on your perception.

7.6.1 Case Study: I once read of a woman who said she lost eight years of her life to psychiatric illness. She said she lost her career, her relationship and her friendships. She attested that her psychiatric illness destroyed her life completely and is to this day battling it to try and beat it. She assumed that because she was failing at careers and relationships, she was thus failing at life. In my opinion her mentality was askew. She did not lose eight years to the illness but rather she learned more about her own individual self in those eight years. She learned about what she could do and what she could not do. She learned about what she could handle and what she could not handle. She was so infected by The Will to Conform that she could only measure her self-esteem in relationships and careers. She had to be succeeding at these facets in order to feel good. Ultimately the only way she would find happiness is if she embraced her illness or if she accepted it as part of her. If only she could turn her psychiatric breakdown into psychiatric break-through. It was not life that was faltering but her perspective and if she did not change her mentality, she would remain unhappy for the foreseeable future. She would still be unhappy in ten years' time, in thirty years' time and it is only when she wakes up one cold morning when she is old and decayed will she realize that she wasted her life being unhappy. One can either wallow in self-pity over their failings in life or they can embrace who they are and try to be grateful to be alive. The choice is yours.

7.7 The life of the average man is far from content. Every day is wave after wave of stress. Deadlines must be met, and targets achieved; partners must be fulfilled, and families must be kept fed. This is the cycle of capitalistic addiction that he goes through. He may succeed in the various facets of life, but the feeling is temporary and subsides after a while. That he accomplishes one day is irrelevant for what about tomorrow or next week or even next month. Every day he wakes up and has to source his happiness from his job and relationship. He is woefully dependent on others for his happiness and this is a game of chance. Thus, freedom if anything is the exclusion of addiction in ones life.

7.8 It is a game that never ceases perhaps until he retires and by then it is too late to enjoy oneself for the best years have slipped by. The means to be happy is to be just grateful for being alive. I know it sounds simplistic, but one must come to realize that they are alive not just in this world, but in this universe. Every day we see the world; we do not see the universe. As such life becomes about relationships and careers. The naked feeling that one is alive in this universe is never perceived.

7.8.1 There is an endemic of people with low self-esteem in capitalistic countries. Despite the fact that they live in a time where they have more money, more food, more warmth and more choices, they are still unhappy. Why is this one may ask? The reason is because one's existence is not enough in this universe. The people of a capitalistic culture must have a desired existence, as in they must be validated by the herd in order to feel good. So, a young man or woman who is rejected by his or her peerage immediately feels discontent in him or herself despite the luxury of life he or she possesses. They then waste many years in trying to appeal to the herd. How does one help such a stricken individual other than suggesting that there is more to life and this universe than being wanted.

7.9 Often anxiety starts from knowing people and them knowing you. A woman whose relationship with her boyfriend ends feels downcast. What if she had never known the man in the first place? She would not have been in a relationship that ended and thus would not feel distraught. Imagine for instance a man who goes off to live on an island. Nobody knows him and thus he cannot be attacked and lives a simple existence. Consequently, the simplest life one can live is not in a relationship but rather as a loner. All our problems stem from being known as do our aspirations. When a man or woman finds the partner of their dreams, they feel warm. That their partner acknowledges them makes them feel content. But what if they are rejected in the future? They feel disconsolate. The price one must pay for being accepted by friends or a partner is that we expose ourselves to potential rejection from these very entities. This ultimately is the risk of being recognised by society.

7.10 Anxiety of Interpretation: All our woes lie in interpretation. Our confidence is determined by how people interpret us. It is not the event that matters but rather how the event is interpreted. As long as we associate ourselves with other people, the threat of a negative opinion off those people stands. It is in doing that we become undone. We do something that is interpreted negatively by the herd and thus we become alienated from the herd. Our lives are thus in a state of turmoil.

7.11 People only start to learn how to live when they grow old. Why? They do so because they no longer are part of the system.

7.12 You are responsible for your own response to life. Tragedy afflicts us all. How you respond to that tragedy is the difference between happiness and self-pity.

7.12.1 No one makes you happy. It is your response to people that makes you happy.

7.12.2 In self-pity we take our existence for granted. People do not realize how fortunate they are to be alive in this universe.

7.12.3 The goal of existential nihilistic therapy is to make people aware of how meaningless life really is. That we are just animals that can speak, that we are just carbon atoms intricately woven together, that we are just a species inhabiting a planet in this indifferent universe. When people realize these things, they negate the capitalist worries that plague them. Thus, the goal of life is to love your existence because you both have the capacity to do so and because you are fortunate to be able to do so. When you fathom how directionless life really is you may just start to be grateful for how lucky you are to be alive.

7.12.4 I read about a man who wanted to be normal. Life was not gratifying him. The Will to Conform was failing him. He then indulged in self-pity to comfort himself. How do you help such a person other than telling them to embrace their existence? It was his perception that was defective and not life itself. I see this repeated often. Those who fail to find love or find a career or find both become so broken. They do not realize how fortunate they are to be alive. Self-pity propelled by the power of The Will to Conform makes their lives miserable.

7.12.5 I have an absolute contempt for those who grovel in self-pity. They cry over their failure to be normal. They lose esteem because they do not have a partner by their side. They don't realize how privileged they are to be alive.

7.12.6 Self-pity is a parasite of capitalism. We automatically deduce that we must have this dream existence. When events conspire against us, we immerse ourselves in reptilian self-absorption. "If only I was this; if only I wasn't that." You cannot see the future if you keep looking behind you.

7.13 Many speak of their road to recovery. But what is recovery? To most it is being normal and this is where they hit a problem. If one tries to be normal, they will not be normal because you distract your unconscious mind from working. When you push your mind too hard it becomes distracted from operating at an effective level. What you do is you immerse yourself in life and hope that you become happy. The problem with some people is that they don't have the skills to do just that. They are caught in a bind.

7.14 Case Study: I read of a man who suffered from severe anxiety. He complained that he just wanted to feel normal. Then in the midst of his self-pity he would blame his doctors and psychologists for not making him happy. It never occurred to him that his problem was rooted not in others but in his own method of thought. So, he would change doctors and change medication in the hope of becoming better. It never dawned on him, to change his mentality. If life is failing you, one must find a life that doesn't fail you. This is an error that many a conformist makes. They can only see one way of living, but they fail at that way of living. They can only see marriage, friendships and work. They then turn to psychiatrists and medication to make them succeed at these facets of life. Then when they don't succeed and remain unhappy, they change psychologists and medication in the desperate hope that they will succeed at these qualities. They then indulge in self-pity: "If only I was this; if only I wasn't that." To even entertain a thought of a different lifestyle is out of the question. Thus, the anxiety is perpetual, and they grow old in a state of despair.

7.15 There isn't a drug around that can suddenly revolutionize your world, because the notion of transforming your world involves everyone within your life suddenly responding as you wish. You are dealing with people who have their own views and opinions. Who act on their own accord and react in ways that upset you. Everyone is under stress but some cope with it better. This is the difference; they endure what life throws at them better. It's not that they don't find the world stressful. They do, but they have the skills and personality to take it on. This is what some anxiety/depression sufferers never comprehend. They want to be like other people. These other people seem to have it all. They have friends and a partner and a good job etc. The anxiety ridden individual wonders how these other people can achieve this, and they can't. And they cry and cry to be able to taste this treasure.

7.16 There are two cures: Remove yourself from the world altogether or change your perspective of the world and if you are really smart you will do both. The anxious ridden individuals are targeting the wrong thing. They say that if they cure their depression, they will function better or so that is the idealistic plan. But the depression won't ever be cured because it is their presence in the world that causes the distress in the first place.

7.17 We live in a world of gratification. People use friends, partners, careers, food, sports teams etc. as a means to be gratified or be entertained. When the individual is not emotionally subsidized by these elements they become anxious. The goal of existentialism or Buddhism is to try and teach man to not be an advocate of gratification. He achieves this through becoming aware of how he lives and thus becomes more tolerant of his boredom. In becoming existentially free he no longer ties is happiness to gratification. He becomes grateful for being alive and thus finds his happiness in his existence.

7.18 One has to begin to accept that they cannot meet the criteria of conformity. In doing this they discover what they can do. The power of The Will to Conform is immense. People automatically see their futures in relationships and careers.

7.19 Alternating one's perception is extremely hard to do because people are schooled on how to live a life from an incredibly young age. They are quietly told they must marry, they must socialise and they must have certain jobs. But these three elements cause such distress. The person then in an effort to protect themselves thinks that it is the disease of anxiety/depression that prevents them from being successful, when it is in fact their own incapability to survive in the world that causes the depression and only when they recognise that they cannot function in the world, will their world improve.

7.20 One must embrace their illness to overcome it. Man needs protection most of all from himself. His own thoughts destroy him.

7.21 One other thing that must be understood is there is a huge contrast between the life we plan on living and the life we do live. So many only see happiness in terms of this dream life wherein they have a partner and a job. But there is a difference between anticipation and execution. One must allow for the uncertainty of the universe.

Species Bias

8.0 That we possess a conscious awareness of our identity and that we can speak ushers us into believing that we are diverse within this universe.

8.1 Our ability to use language in particular automatically elevates us to a level above other animals.

8.1.1 Thus a pattern in life begins to take shape.

8.2 That we are intelligent animals endeavours to make us believe that we make our own conscious choices when in fact we do not.

8.3 Language in a sense misleads us from the realities of the world. Life becomes about the two-dimensional aspects of relationships and careers and we say to ourselves as speaking humans that this is a worthy life.

8.3.1 We fail to realize that just as a shark uses it sense of smell to hunt prey or a bat uses echolocation to navigate, man uses language as a tool to survive in this world.

8.3.2 It's just that possessing the tool of language makes him unconsciously believe that he is above other species.

8.3.3 He says to himself unconsciously: "I am the only animal that can speak; thus, I must be above all other animals."

8.3.4 We thus relegate all other animals to a lower level than ourselves and because of this we abuse and slaughter them in their billions so that we can fuel economies.

8.3.5 And we do not express shame or remorse because of this species bias. The pigs in the slaughterhouse are pigs that mean little to us. Thus, we kill them and consume them without anxiety.

8.4 The other problem is that we are in denial over our ability to accept that we are just animals. The successful man or the attractive woman do not want to be told that they are animals. They do not want to be told that they are just a species that can talk and that is under incredible pressure to procreate.

8.5 Both men and women do not like being told that they are animals. They have an ill-informed opinion that by being human they are something above an animal. They pride themselves on their looks and that they are built in the image of god. To relegate themselves to the same level as a pig in an abattoir is to shatter their self-confidence about their standing in the world.

8.6 That we have developed god in the image of man is a testament to this. We unconsciously feel we are special on this planet, when it is in fact our ability to speak that gives birth to our perceived superiority.

The Paradox of Hedonism

9.0 Happiness is not something that can be consciously acquired. It relies on one's unconscious to be stimulated to be realized.

9.0.1 People automatically deduce that if they meet the constraints of conformity, they will procure the elusive happiness. They assume that marriage and the esteemed career will yield jubilation. It may, but then again it may not.

9.1 A relationship and a career both involve liaising with other people. But to deal with other people is to deal in uncertainty. People by default are irrational and unpredictable. They don't always do what the individual wishes they would do. The only certainty in life is uncertainty.

9.1.1 We are subject to the interpretation of the other person and that interpretation can be negative.

9.1.2 Thus one can see how following the script of conformity is not an assured method to procure happiness.

9.1.3 Furthermore we put ourselves under severe pressure consciously when we follow the template of conformity. That we expect to become happy distracts us from actually being happy.

9.2 This is the paradox of hedonism. The more one tries to be happy, the more it eludes them.

9.3 Take for instance the man I alluded to earlier who said he wanted to feel like a normal person. By this he meant he wished to feel happy like other people. He looked at other people within his circle and saw them enjoying life and gaining promotions in work. What did not occur to him was that the more he yearned for happiness, the more it escaped his grasp. The more he longed to become happy through the methodology of conforming, the more pressure he put on his mind to be happy and hence happiness escaped him. The more he tried to be happy in the form of a relationship or work, the more he actually distracted himself from unconsciously being happy in these things.

9.3.1 The problem though was that he was in a bind. Society had inbuilt into him that the path to happiness was through conformity (relationships and careers). He had no other choice but to persevere on this path.

9.3.2 The Buddhist methodology of being grateful for being alive was not an option. He was so conditioned from life to only see happiness in terms of a relationship and a career.

9.3.3 Imagine it like this: One watches a film on the expectation that it will be enjoyable and if the film is good enough it provides a degree of pleasure for the observer. One cannot say prior to watching the film, that the film will make them happy. That is consciously expecting to be happy, which distracts your unconscious from actually being happy. All one can do is watch the film and hope they become happy through watching it. But it is not guaranteed. Now apply this to the individual who strives to be happy through conforming. He or she consciously attests that if only they had a certain life, they would be happy. "If only I was married, I would be happy; if only I was popular, I would be happy; if only I had a good job, I would be happy." But through saying such things they consciously distract their unconscious from actually experiencing happiness. It stands to reason that those individuals who gain happiness from conforming, do so without realizing it. That they are not expecting to become happy through conforming essentially means they experience happiness.

9.4 One cannot try to be happy consciously. The more you say to yourself: "I want to be happy," the more you disturb your unconscious from actually being happy.

9.5 Thus there are only two forms of happiness: A) Happiness through gratification and B) Happiness through gratitude.

9.5.1 Most of the world falls into category (A). When they are positively gratified, they feel emotionally good. But the high wears off and a new high is requested.

9.5.2 This category was defective in the man that I mentioned. He couldn't be emotionally gratified by life and thus felt anxious.

9.5.3 Furthermore he was blind to gratitude. He was so conditioned on system (A) that being appreciative for just being alive never occurred to him. Thus, he spent his days in an anxious agony craving to feel happy like other people.

9.6 If you can be taught to be emotionally gratified by life you can be taught to be thankful for being alive. It all depends on your perception.

9.6.1 Now it takes retraining one's unconsciousness to perceive life in a different manner and it takes time. But gradually one begins to view life in a new light. So instead of waking up to be emotionally subsidized by life, one wakes up and appreciates life. To change one's life, one need not actually change their life, but rather only change their perception and that will change their life.

9.7 So many commoditize their happiness. By this I mean they use the image of being happy through marriage and careers to attest that they are happy. This happiness consists of being married, having a family, succeeding at a job, looking respectable etc. Is one actually happy or are they just pretending to be happy?

9.8 An obese woman who is not valued by the herd immediately says to herself that she is unhappy. She says so because the herd does not subsidize her. She ties her happiness to being vindicated by the herd. She needs to be endorsed by society in order to feel of worth and this is her fatal mistake. Thus, she says: "If only I was attractive. Then I would be happy." Another example is a man who because he is single castigates himself for his perceived failure. The herd doesn't like single men by default and in his naivety, he believes them. He thus continuously says that he cannot be content until he is in a relationship.

9.9 The paradox of success: The more you try to consciously accomplish at a particular avenue of life, the less you accomplish. The more you try to consciously impress people the less you do. The more you try to be consciously happy the less happy you become. You are consciously distracting your unconscious mind. All these things depend on the unconscious to be of worth. But people make the mistake of consciously trying to be happy when it is unconscious in nature. They then chase the labels of happiness thinking that they will make them happy.

9.10 What one must remember is that no one can consciously try to be happy. All one can do is unconsciously saturate themselves in a relationship, a job, a book, a film, a sports match and hope that they become happy. But it is not guaranteed.

9.11 A naïve person says: I am going to enjoy my life; an intelligent person says: I am going to live and hope that I enjoy my life.

9.12 Case Study: I read of man who complained to a psychologist that he was failing to find a job because of his poor interview technique. What transpired was that the man was frantic to get a job and before each interview he would say to himself "I must do well at this interview," or "I really want this job and must do a good interview." The psychologist explained to him that by saying these things repeatedly he was putting himself under so much pressure to perform and as such was consciously trying to impress the employer rather than letting his unconscious instinct do the work for him. The psychologist concluded by suggesting that at the next interview instead of the man wanting the job, try to have the mentality of not wanting that particular job. So instead of thinking: "I really want this job," say "I really don't want this job." The thinking of the psychologist was that if the man didn't want the job, he would not put himself under pressure to perform and thus would be more relaxed at the interview and would give a better account of himself through his instinctive response.

9.12.2 Thus a man or a woman looks to the future and sees themselves married and working in a good career and automatically assumes that they will be happy in such a system. But they fail to realize that happiness can never be planned. This is a mistake many an individual who suffers from the conformist anxiety makes. They start to dream and in this dream they are married, working and above all else happy. Ergo they expect to be happy in such a procedure. By having this mentality, they are consciously putting themselves under pressure to be happy, which as it transpires is counter-productive because this actually distracts their unconscious from operating and hence destroys any semblance of happiness one could possess. Thus a system of unhappiness prevails: They are unhappy because they fail to conform; but when they try to conform they meet further unhappiness often in the form of anxiety.

9.13 Conformity stipulates that they marry and work and as such they automatically assume these facets will endeavour to make them happy. They think: "If only I was married I would be happy." "If only I had that job, I would be happy." They assume that those two things will oblige to make them happy and this is a huge mistake to make.

9.13.1 As such they enter into these arrangements and never become happy. Their anticipation is never met with concrete happiness.

9.14 One often hears psychologists say that the best mentality to have is to not expect much. So, if one was going to see a film or on a date, the best attitude to have is to have little expectation of that film or date. The reason they say this is because when you are not expecting much from the event, you do not consciously put pressure on yourself to enjoy the event.

9.15 Robert M Pirsig said it best: "To live only for some future goal is shallow. It's the sides of the mountain that sustain life, not the top." What he essentially means is that dreaming of the perfect future life in the mould of relationships and careers is a huge mistake to make. Society automatically looks to the future and says: "In ten years' time I will be married and at this particular stage of my career." Furthermore, through actively saying this, they assume they will be happy in ten years' time when they are married and at a certain stage of their career. Thus, it is both foolish and a waste of life to forgo happiness in the present on the assumption that you will be happy in the future. One must also understand that this dream life may not actually materialise as one planned or hoped. What Pirsig was basically conveying to the reader is that one must try to be happy now to be happy in the future. Don't neglect the present in favour of a dream.

9.16 As youths we are guilty of dreaming. Both men and women plan for their marriage thirty years before they get married. They plan their lives before they have even lived. They assert that they will be happy when they get married.

9.16.1 Ultimately the people who are happy in life are the ones who are not desperate to be happy. One cannot be happy; they can only experience happiness.

Existential Freedom

10.0 The psychologically healthy individual is caught in a capitalist web. He has been brainwashed from childhood to want certain things and to operate a certain way. He thus becomes an agent of gratification. One's freedom is thus their ability to see this invisible imprisonment and to then make a decision.

10.1 Can people not see that they are hopelessly reliant on another person for their self-esteem? Does one not believe that to be free one must prize their loneliness?

10.2 You cannot lose if you have nothing to lose. People depend on friendships, relationships and careers to make them happy. But what materializes when these things don't make them content? They are addicted to friendships, relationships and careers and when the addict does not get his high, he becomes depressed.

10.3 Your existential freedom is your gratefulness to be alive. It is to appreciate every day, every second. The goal of existence is to formulate your own philosophy on how best to live that existence. Don't just accept The Will to Conform as your system to live. Liberate yourself; make every day the greatest day of your life.

10.4 People are so induced on normality that they just accept it as normal. They are so conditioned on what is conventional that they cannot see it as madness. Like I asserted earlier if intelligent life were to pay a visit and observe humankind they would see pattern. They would almost deduce that we are tissue engineered machines such is our predictability. They would see billions of people who assert to themselves that they cannot love their existence unless they fall in love. They would see billions of people who believe in a divine power. They would see billions of people who pour portions of their disposable income into corporations who care not a dime for them. The intelligent life would conclude that we are insane but because billions of people want to fall in love or follow a religion or follow a sports team, that insanity becomes normalized.

10.5 The very fact that we unconsciously believe ourselves to be intelligent means we do not question the system. Thus, qualities such as falling in love, believing in god, supporting football teams and following famous people are just casually accepted as normal.

10.6 The sole purpose of one's life is to discover their freedom. An existentially aware individual recognises the system of conformity and how it blinds that individual to the truths of the universe.

10.6.1 We live in an age of luxury. We have enough food, enough warmth and enough shelter. Yet we remain unhappy. Why are we so unhappy despite the richness we possess? Part of the reason is because existence is not enough for people of a capitalist upbringing. They must have a desired existence.

Man must be the only animal who is afraid of what other animals think of him. He lives in fear of being negatively labelled and thus leverages his self-esteem on being positively endorsed by society.

10.7 Don't think of your house, your town, your country, your continent or even your planet. Think of how lucky you are to be alive in this universe. Be absolutely in love with your own freedom, your own individuality and your own existence.

10.7.1 How beautiful it is to taste existence. But the common man does not appreciate his life. He is so caught up in the two-dimensional aspect of life: Relationships and careers. So much in fact that he is visionless to who he is and to the universe.

10.8 Do not measure your self-worth in friendships, relationships or careers. These are systems of navigating, not *the* system to journey through life. Be grateful for being alive. Make your willingness not to depend on positive affirmation from the herd your self-esteem.

10.9 Contemporary thought has us believe that in order to love our life we must be loved by another. It is an immature and naïve way of approaching life. Nihilism teaches that one can love life without being loved. Love your universe in spite of its indifference; love yourself in spite of your faults.

10.10 You can be a disciple of gratification or you can just be happy to be alive. The choice is yours. One should wake up each day thankful to exist in this universe and one day you will. Hopefully, it won't be when it is too late to start living.

10.11 Death is not the greatest tragedy of existence but rather the misuse of one's existence is.

10.12 Existential Nihilistic Therapy teaches its disciples about the universe and their place in it; it teaches that each person is just an animal composed of trillions of atoms; it teaches that man is just a species that can use language to see. But most of all it teaches that one should wake up each day grateful for being alive and that one's existence is the greatest achievement in this indifferent dark environment.

10.13 The opposite to conformity is not anarchy but rather an apathetic rebellion. To rebel against The Will to Conform is your freedom.

10.14 Case Study: Irvin Yalom once said that a cancer patient told him that she only learned how to live when she was terminally ill. What did she mean by that? What she meant was that it was only when she had a couple of months to live did she learn to appreciate life and stop worrying. You see we are most deceived when most alive. Life becomes two dimensional. It becomes about relationships and careers. Thus, we worry about not being in love or the next day at work. What existential nihilistic therapy endeavours to do is to try and make you aware of your place in this universe and through doing this the anxieties that accompany day to day living perish. The woman who Irvin Yalom treated stopped worrying about love and her job as soon as she realized she did not have much more time to live. She finally accepted herself in this universe. She began to appreciate the world much more. She became indebted for just being alive. The trick is to have this mentality when you are young and free.

So instead of worrying about someone you like or problems at work, you alter your perception to become harmonious with the universe. Thus, when one realizes how fortunate they are to exist not in their city or country or even planet, but in this despairing universe, their anxieties become purged and they finally begin to love their existence. The indifferent universe can be your death sentence or if you allow it, it can be your salvation.

10.15 Your freedom as a human is your ability to love your life. Your liberty in part is your willingness to defy your unconscious will to conform. The most privileged part of existence is existence.

10.15.1 Starve yourself to appreciate your food; freeze yourself to appreciate your warmth; gaze into the starry night sky to appreciate how good it is to be alive.

10.15.2 Gratitude is the only cure.

10.16 You often hear people on New Year's Eve hoping that the next year will bring them reward. They hope that life will treat them well. What they don't realize is that they can make the New Year rewarding if they just change their thoughts.

10.17 Your Existential Freedom is this: Defy education, do not become a slave to other people; defy evolution, do not become a slave to sexual gratification; defy your peers, do not become a slave to the herd; and accept your boredom, do not use life as an escape.

10.17.1 Instead of telling people to see the world, we should teach them to see the universe. They may just then begin to honour life.

10.18 The best psychologist in your life is yourself. One must turn their self-pity into gratitude. Society is taught to find another person to complete them. They are never taught to find themselves.

10.19 Stop thinking: "If only I was this; if only I wasn't that." Don't let the self-pity carve your conscience bare. If you love life, it will love you back. Embrace who you are. This includes your faults and your failings.

10.20 You have a choice: Do you want to make other people happy or do you want to make yourself happy?

10.21 I once read about a woman who was asked what it would be like spending Christmas alone. She retorted that she was not alone because solitude was a great and trusted companion. This woman was existentially free. She was not dependent on another person or persons to make her content. She was not an addict of life but rather she was addicted to her own existence and her own sense of being alive.

10.22 One must be existentially awoken. Right now, as you read these notes you are living on a planet that revolves around a parent star in a universe whose size is incomprehensible. Right now, the carbon atoms in your body are being bonded together by the strong and weak nuclear forces. We are so blinded by the conventional life. We only see relationships and careers. The universe and the atoms that constitute our bodies may as well not exist. If you can see the beauty in life and in the universe you will be happy.

Final Word

Often, I gaze into the night sky and wonder why there is something and not nothing? Why do the planets exist? Why does space time exist? Why do atoms exist? In pondering such a question I feel a sense of gladness at being alive. I then realize how fortunate I am to be alive in this universe where life and reason are seldom found together. The two-dimensional aspect of existence in marriage and careers casts a veil over our conscience. We become so consumed by both that we refute the greater realities of this world. Life becomes about working and servicing relationships. We are gifted through language with reason, yet we often decline to use it. It brings to mind what the oil tycoon John D Rockefeller once said: "I want a nation of workers, not thinkers." Ultimately society through work and relationships forgets that they are living on a planet or that they are an animal.

The goal of existential nihilism is to set man free. The goal is to rid him of worry. It is only when we have days to live do we truly appreciate life. With these and previous notes I try to offer an alternative model of living to that of conformity. I do so because I passionately believe that it is a more concrete model of which to become happy. Fundamentally one's substance for existence should be to find their freedom. Life goes by so quickly. The days crystallize into months and the months to years. To spend your time worrying or in a state of anxiety is a total waste of your life. Change your mind-set. Change how you perceive your life and you will change your life. To do this one must unlearn what they have learned.

Through systematic education your mind has been psychologically contorted to operate in a certain method. Thus, society is consumed with love and careers. Ones liberty thus lies in challenging this system. Be prepared to question the very people you love. My philosophy is that the individual conceives of their own philosophy on how best to live. As I said earlier, to own yourself, to dictate your calling, is the greatest luxury of life. Do not just casually accept conformity as a means to live. Set yourself free in the despairing moonlight. Discover your own path on how best to conquer the mountain that is life and don't settle for the worn-out trail of conformity.